Hopes, Dreams & Visions per God

TAWNY MAE HARRIS

HOPES, DREAMS & VISIONS PER GOD

iUniverse books may be ordered through booksellers or by contacting:

iUniverse
1663 Liberty Drive
Bloomington, IN 47403
www.iuniverse.com
844-349-9409

Because of the dynamic nature of the Internet, any web addresses or links contained in this book may have changed since publication and may no longer be valid. The views expressed in this work are solely those of the author and do not necessarily reflect the views of the publisher, and the publisher hereby disclaims any responsibility for them.

Any people depicted in stock imagery provided by Getty Images are models, and such images are being used for illustrative purposes only. Certain stock imagery © Getty Images.

ISBN: 978-1-6632-4306-5 (sc)
ISBN: 978-1-6632-4307-2 (e)

Print information available on the last page.

iUniverse rev. date: 07/28/2022

Dedicated to a great friend that died
from COVID-19 – Anne.

Hopes, Dreams & Visions per God

What do these dreams mean?

Dream # 1

I am at Ponderosa working. I go to the bathroom & people keep trying to get in. It is a half door. I put my pretty purse on the shelf & ask the manager for a job. I am graduating college with an Assoc. in Arts & Applied Science with good grades & have 7 years experience as waitress. The manager & I look at our pretty diamond rings. She gets up from the table. There is a very old lady that says pine wine. The lady manager comes back & says "Mae, I have nothing more to say." I say thank you anyway, leave & get into my car. I almost turn it over. I am walking a tiny black dog on a leash by Kentucky Fried Chicken. There is a girl with long flowing black hair. She says she has wolf hair. I said Ponderosa won't hire me. There is a rattlesnake & a puppy & a rabbit. I am afraid that the rattlesnake is going to bite the dog. I am walking in the dark down McCoy Avenue to go home where Mom is with my beloved sheep dog, Levi. The rabbit is following me & I look back to see if the rattlesnake is following me. I wake up. I am wearing a long red, white & blue medium skirt & a long red shirt.

Dream # 2

I am in my blue bedroom eating a gay girl's pussy. She cums. I am not gay. Cats are flowing & trying to eat my favorite white cat with gold eye's food. I am in the York plant with my gay brother. There is a defeated basketball & he disappears. Next, I am in a cabin with white sheets saying to the lawyer "Where's my brother?!" "Where's my brother?!" Was he murdered? The lawyer says yes he was. Next, I am in a cabin setting a table with silver ware & there is a pretty girl. My white cat, Wrangler, is running out the door. I wake up.

Dream # 3

I am in my bedroom asleep. An evil spirit says Holly, Holly, Holly. I say I am not Holly!

Dream # 4

I am in a dark place. My best Scorpio girlfriend Forgiveness that went to prison for counterfeiting 20's & D.V.I.'s is dead & is in a body bag on a truck getting ready to go to Heaven. I am getting an orange drink out of a vending machine & they need me here for something.

Dream # 5

Forgiveness & I are hiding behind the porch stoop & there is a huge fire breathing green mardi gra dragon after us.

Dream # 6

I climb thru spider's cob webs. I am in a dark lake laughing & Forgiveness is vain strolling on the bank. A huge pit viper is swimming down the lake straight towards me. I try to hit the snake but it jumps up & bites me on the neck. Did I die?

Dream # 7

I am in a dark lake with many tiny black snakes. Maebell, Mom Loyal Dedication's best red headed brown-eyed rich friend is in a boat & saves me.

Dream # 8

I come in the living room & Mom has a gun underneath her robe. I chop off her head with a sword before she shoots & kills me in self defense.

Dream # 9

I dream the grim ugly reaper gives me the middle - yea finger.

Dream # 10

I dream my gay brother beloved Micah are boarding a plane.
I am signing papers & my ticket is A-13 seat on the plane.
I have had nothing but bad luck since I've had this dream.

Dream # 11

I have all kinds of baby dreams. I dreamed I was walking from Forgiveness's Mother's house, Ms. Judgement that burned down from the ground. I have 3 children - 2 girls & a boy. The boy turns into a celery stalk & withers up.

Dream # 12

I dreamed deceased cousin Faith was in a dark & evil place. Rebekkah her sister had a boy & named it a weird name. There are cute kittens & Faith places a small bottle of perfume in my hand.

Dream # 13

My black Aveo car Panther gets stolen. I keep losing my cars in my dreams. Gay girls are trying to touch me. I get on the phone to the police, "You had better find my car!" Don't mam me!" Fat Gracie Bathsheba bitch is eating. We are in a bar & mother has been drinking. She says my car is somewhere in Texas. I slam the lighted candle down & break it. I cannot take anymore hell!

Dream # 14

Mother is drunk & is in jail. I go to visit her. Did she go to hell for drinking, shooting herself, hanging around gays, atheists Judge Wonderful Tahiti & his wife Mourn, making fun of Jesus. Rainbows were everywhere when she died of throat cancer on February 18, 1994. I saw the dark death angels & Uncle Protection a Taurus came back for her.

Dream # 15

I am at home & I tell Mom I am saving $10.00 out of my check. I go to True/Trust/Truth's house. It is a nice red brick house & the yard needs mowing. I go outside & her boyfriend with red hair & brown eyes, big is standing there. I ask him what his name is. He says Steve Harris & I tell him my name Mae is in the Bible 5 times. I go inside & he is cleaning up the kitchen. True/Trust/Truth a beautiful Scorpio says, "I am going to get something to eat. Do you want to go?" I say yes & I wake up.

Dream # 16

Uncle Protection rapes me from behind in the house on Scott Street. I hate him for that!

Dream # 17

There is a dark haired child on the white bedspread in my room asleep. Is it a boy or a girl? Brennan Scott. Is the child retarded & will it fall off the bed? My grandmother Wonderful Strength that I loves appears & loves this child. I have my make-up on & look pretty. Where is the father of the child?

Dream # 18

I am in a recovery room. Mother is with me. I have an I.V. in my leg after giving childbirth to a baby girl. Did I have a C-section? The baby girl has brown hair & big blue eyes - Fawn Christiana Mae & we bond immediately. Who was the father? I am glad I had this baby. Mom is right by my side.

Dream # 19

I dreamed I popped my beloved tabby cat, Thunder Theology Curiosity, in the mouth with a rubber band- a very cruel, inhumane thing to do.

Dream # 20

I dreamed my black soul sister, Cheer, died & she did die of an unknown disease with a feeding tube in a nursing home. I do not understand why we have to die. Am I psychic? Am I clairvoyant? I am kin to the sleeping prophet Edgar Cayce by marriage. He was kin to my favorite Uncle Humor - a Libra. Cheer was born on Valentine's Day - a fellow Aquarius. I cry every time I think of her. She was funny & she was computer smart.

Dream # 21

I dreamed I was in a wheelchair paralyzed from the waist down right behind Gracie Bathsheba at Shop-a-Lot # 666 # 999. Why did you let that "B" run all over you? What if you fell off that ladder & broke a hip, back, or arm? You should have sued their asses off for telling lies on you, slander, you burned down the hospital, strung up black people. That does not even make sense. You don't even believe in slavery.

Dream # 22

I dreamed Mother was going to knock the hell out of me. I said I think that is child abuse; so, she tickled me instead. I cannot stand to be tickled touched by a woman. I cannot stand to have an arm put around me. Hugs are okay. Satan had better not touch me - not today Satan. Jayden "Care" Arthur, Asst. Manager, thought I was awesome. Young, dumb, & full of cum.

Dream # 23

I dreamed I accidently kissed a black person on the lips - Heaven a switchboard operator at Camel Carriers Trucking Company. Yuck! Gross! That makes me want to puke. I loved this black lady: but, I do not want to kiss her on the lips. It is only a strange dream Mae. Halo was the other black lady I loved - my blue sister. You have to do what you have to do. Camel Carriers Trucking Company moved to the sunshine state. I worked there for 17 glorious years as switchboard operator & money desk clerk - liaison to Com Data. Gift/Gifted a computer programmer hippy - a good Pisces is dead at 49 & keeps coming back to me in dreams. Who is Gandolf the wizard & who is Aragon? I want to sit down at her grave & talk to her. What happened when you died? Do you still play the guitar & sing? Greenpeace- Rescue a cat. She was a good person.

Dream # 24

The grossest dream I have ever had was this young boy who I did not know his name was slinging sticky gross cum all over me. I slung the cum off my hand. Did I meet him at the laundry mat? What if you had a dick Mae? Would you masterbate? Will masturbation cause you to go blind? I hope Hopes, Dreams, & Visions per God sells. Hope flourishes. Doubt flies. Hope was a nurse practitioner shrink who was a quack & I hope she dies from COVID-19. Dr. Sam. I can't stand the Scorpio bitch! She does not want to listen to your problems & she will call the E.P.O. on you if you move. I hope she gets fired for the lies she told on me when she incarcerated me at 50 in Jebosite Haven. You were handing out Prayer Warrior books at Zion, Egypt clinic, slept on the couch cause you are afraid you'd be raped, went to the door naked. All lies!

Between the deaths of gay lesbian alcoholic Ecclesiastes & Hope's nephew that was manic-depressive & prayed for me sending me cards, I am devastated. Here is one of the deceased boy's poems.

"A Piece of Peace"
I found a piece of peace today,
Just found it here along the way,
Not by stray did it appear

Perhaps by chance or coincidence
Maybe fate allowed that glimpse
My soul must relate
I grabbed it. I saved it.
I could not understand it,
Yet knew what it meant
Soon came others
At times several in a day
Miracles of knowing
Found best in the simplest way
Like a book of symbols & numbers
Thinking as a child I can sometimes read. But fate alone, this contentment cannot be. This peace is grace. This peace is grace, Yes, now I see. But wait, there is more. This was a piece of me. I love you religious gay boy!
Rest in peace. Follow God's white gloved hand everywhere.

Dream # 25

The air-conditioner is not working you will go straight to hell for shooting yourself Mae. Read Leviticus. Homosexuality is an abomination of the Lord. You had better not turn your back on God. Prayer is the wireless connection. I had a dream that I had a brand new nice house. There were a collie in one bedroom, 2 shitz zus in another bedroom, & a big black dog that let himself in the back door. Amos & King of the Jews from Shop-a-Lot # 666 # 999 are at my house & I am reading bar codes off of clothes.

Dream # 26

I dream I am in a car with 2 pit bulls & I cover my face; so, they will not bite me. I walk up these stairs to a house & fall off.

Dream # 27

I dream & I am in clear cool water & there is a current. I climb a very high platform & I am going to jump off in the lake & wake up.

Dream # 28

Early to bed. Early to rise makes a man healthy, wealthy & wise per famous Ben Franklin will all my dreams come true? The kidney sweetheart doctor & nurses, Joseph Abraham, the 88 year old plumber treat me like a queen goddess of the office.

Is God trying to tell me something while I am asleep? Is death a blessing? I am not ready to go. All girlfriend Charity does is put me down. I believe in dreams. Only scarred lives save. Dream big - claim big things. Not today Satan. Jesus is my Man. You have to be a bit too kind in this world to be kind enough.

My favorite dream is that I am living in a dirty farmhouse in Israel. There are yellow flowers everywhere & I have a gray speckled horse & a white horse named ghost. There is a collie on the front porch. Aunt Wisdom, Uncle Humor, & Mom Loyal Dedication visit me in spirit. Mom goes to the basement. I hug the good-looking farm hand & I am very happy.

I put on a black wig to go to the bakery store because Israel does not like Americans. Witches are cutting my hair.

Dream # 29

I dream I am on a planet. There are huge snowy owls everywhere. I am on a plane & I look very pretty with my long ash brown hair. The plane does not take off. What do the tall white snowy owls mean?

Dream # 30

I am on a plane & I am pissed that my gay brother Micah is on the plane with me. The plane dives straight down & lets Micah off with our mother. I am in the clinic with white pants & navy scrub shirt on. There are nurses in the hall gossiping. I do not gossip. I am late in a nurses class to take a test with my social security number. A voice tells me - you know the answers.

Dream # 31

When I was a child in kindergarten at Hebrew Tabernacle Episcopal Church, I would have a dream about a big bright red dragon that would scare me & I would climb in my mother's bed.

Dream # 32

When I was a child, I dreamed I was on a planet holding on with my fingers & hands & my brother Micah stomped on them & I would fall off. Is Micah a devil worshipper? That was mean. Do gay people go straight to hell? Are they born that way or is it a choice. Read Leviticus. Mae has had 5 nervous breakdowns– CRAZY CHECK 16-19-21-24-50 – Our Lady of Mercy, House of Horrors/Wax & Jebosite Haven. Do you believe in reincarnation & past lives? Mae is now on disability for manic-depression, paranoid schizophrenia & home kidney dialysis. COVID-19 is getting on my last nerve. Wear pink for heart, soul, & love. Did gay lesbian alcoholic Ecclesiastes go to hell? She will get her revenge for Joy, Happiness, & Canaan. Vengeance is mine saith the Lord. God is a jealous God. Where lies the soul of Adam Lot?

Dream # 33

I was having a depression crying fit because Simon the artist was using me for money. Jesus was hovering over me & He could not do anything. I jump up & take 2 shots of Swedish Absolut vodka chasing it with water & feel better. I turn in the dining room & there is an angel in a navy calico dress. I could not see her face. It was a bright light. The angel said - Low & behold, I am an angel. Your troubles will be laid low & next time drink water. I am drinking the hell out of water.

Dream # 34

Deceased Ecclesiastes from a heart attack means star & you had better be careful what you wish for. You just might get it. You may regret it. God is coming back to judge the living & the dead. You Mae have been an angel since God talked to you. You want to touch Jesus's robe. Your faith has healed you. There is power in the blood. You want sympathy. Mom Loyal Dedication called you poor pitiful pearl. You will never love again - Lady Gaga. Did Robin Williams go straight to hell for hanging himself? Scorpios are mean & they rule the sex loins. There is an onyx cross on your back. You should have married Jordan Thaddeus. You are with Billy Graham. Where there is hate let me sow love per St. Francis of Assisi. How many times has God saved your life - Live-in-forever-eternity. How many times did St. Peter eater rape you with rubbers. His dick is nasty.

Why is LEO girlfriend R.N. nurse deceased Persistence haunting you? Are these dreams real? You made a deal with God - no drinking & driving. He said yes. Mescaline is a very religious drug. You thanked God everyday for that Charity Hang man is coming down from the gallows & I don't have very long. You had better wash your mouth out with soap Mae. Look what Sasha did - she called 911 to bring her food & vodka. She got put in jail. Jail is hell! I have been in jail twice in 1982.

Feed the ghost! You will never take the # 666 of the beast. Weep went straight to hell for saying she thought I shot Mom. I have never touched a gun.

I am sitting at the dining room table with my florescent orange coat on after remodel at Shop-a-Lot. 2 cherub angels appear in a white cloud with trumpets & say it is time to go lifting my spirit up to Heaven & giving me a new spirit cloak. All I have left is a body & peace came over me. These angels are flipping me out! Did I go up in the rapture? I told America personnel manager at Shop-a-Lot when I was getting my check. Is my house Tara adobe abode haunted? Is my life in danger? My house got broken into & they stole jewelry, lighters. St. Mary's sacrament pic. The young & dumb police did not do anything! They could have raped, murdered me, set my house on fire, killed my beloved sweet cat Theo. They broke down the utility room door. You cannot live you life in fear. Fear streaked at Zion, Egypt High School, was hung like a horse, good-looking, went to Lagrange for armed robbery & drowned in a lake. How did he drown?

He was an avid swimmer - butterfly, breast, free style. LATER he would write. Tie a 100 yellow ribbons around that old oak tree to be released from prison if you still want me.

Dream # 35

I dreamed I was in a lake with a nose diamond minding my own business. Jeremiah & Isabella were there. Somebody was trying to drown me. I kick them & come up to the surface in the yellowish - green lake water. I get out & go to the top of the hill & look down there. Then, I am hungry & want something to eat - a hamburger or something. What does this dream mean? LOVE casteth out all FEAR. His sister LOVE o'd on morphine. 60 minutes came down from New York City. Her face was cyan blue, no make-up, & they did not fix her black hair in 1974. Was she murdered? She's the one who got me on mescaline, acid L. S. D. I o'd on valium, had my stomach pumped. Get these spiders off me. I am Dutch. My bitchy mother put me on the 6th floor mental ward & I went to Our Lady of Mercy mental hospital tutored by nuns for 3 months. I am so scared of purple rain - Prince. I cried my eyes out! Angels are everywhere! My guardian angel's name is Caleb which means dog. Gift/Gifted my pretty deceased guitarist good Pisces friend got busted for drugs. 60 minutes came down & Zion, Egypt was on T.V. Gift/Gifted was a computer programmer at Camel Carriers Trucking Company for 30 years, cat rescue, Catholic & went straight to Heaven # 7 at 49. I keep having dreams about her. We were just like sisters & I miss her so much. We used to smoke pot together &

I got a pipe from Folz City. What if your child did drugs, Mae? What would you do? Your mother shot herself & went straight to hell for that. All she says is you make me sick. I am a martyr & a scapegoat & you will be better off without Canaan. Tell Micah & Joy to eat SHIT & die for putting me in Jebosite Haven at 50.

How many times have you been abandoned, lied on, betrayed & stabbed in the back - verbal abuse. You have been trespassed on. Look what Trespasser/Transgressions did to you. He pulled out his big dick & you poured sprite all over it. He owned a BBQ place & fired you. Mom said that was okay. That's when a good boyfriend shot himself in the head & was found on the side of the road. God said He was sorry for scaring the living SHIT out of you. Today is Friday the 13th. I am very superstitious. My air conditioner broke - more bad luck said the duck. Tell these voices to shut the _____ up! Godspell next door neighbor is a beautiful Capricorn like a 2nd mother. I love her. Her son Freewill is a jerk & is horny. Do I have the shining? All work & no play makes Jack a dull boy. Red rum. 5-13-22. Ring a bell to get the evil spirits out of your house Tara adobe abode. Feed Juju the black cat & Theo. Sneezing makes me _____ing mad!

An eye for an eye - a tooth for a tooth. Open your ears to hear God's loving voice. Pray for the financial waiver. Dr. Blessings is a kidney specialist sweetheart & the nurses are treating you like Queen Goddess of the office. The wicked get no rest. Canaan says you ought to take the Old Testament & New Testament & wipe your butt with it. Sleep in peace. Peace was a classy art teacher - agnostic.

There is a God! LOVE is never having to say you're sorry per Ali McGraw & Ryan O'Neal. Beware of Geminis. Look what happened to John Lenon. Karma is going to get you. You had better fast & you had better pray. Atheists go straight to hell! Mourn & Wonderful Tahiti. Why did God make bats & rats? Roaches, fleas? Canaan is a narcissiant & a psychopath. Somebody is stalking you. One flew over the cukoo's nest. You should have sued Shop-a-Lot # 666 # 999.

What is your sign? These voices tell you what to do & put you down. You are enabling Ecclesiastes. That typing, shorthand college teacher was the greatest lady that ever lived. She could not say no in the mirrow & got scholarships for everybody. God is dead is the evilest song you have ever heard by Black Sabbath. Is God crazy- God is pure LOVE. You do not get along with Cancers. Peace was in a horrible car wreck. The mack truck driver lost his leg. Why did God make germs? Your mother said she was sorry calling you thunder thighs & fat hog. You did not accept her apology. Mom & Persistance are haunting your ass off! Tell God a joke & make you laugh. There were 3 lawyers who died & went up to the pearly gates. The 1st lawyer gave St. Peter a candle & he let him in. The 2nd lawyer gave him a bell & St. Peter let him in. The 3rd lawyer hung up a pair of women's panties, underwear. St. Peter raised his eyebrows. The 3rd lawyer said they're Carols. Laughter is good medicine. Laughter was my beloved step mother who was a Libra & died at 91. Prayer is the wireless connection. How bad did you hate your mother! Go live with your father, Perseverence. He did not give a hoot about you! You are dying from home kidney dialysis & you had better not say God ____. How bad did you hate that crazy man at soldiers of the Cross that went to prison for stabbing his crazy son. You had better not sell the house or have children per Aunt Wisdom who was just like Mammy. You are a slut, Mae! J. C. sold the gas station for $700,000 & could not stand black soul sister Cheer who passed. He called her a nigger. It is so evil to kill, shoot yourself. Forgiveness, my best Scorpio friend is going to yank that dead mother _____er up who shot himself in front of his wife & child & beat the SHIT out of him. That is just plum mean. Mae is petrified of clowns - IT - the scariest movie I have ever seen. Oh, my God! I was in church & God's voice said you were wicked go. It was after the dreaded ice storm. Moses deacon said you are NOT wicked & you are a great lady. I love this 92 old religious man! Think positive & positive things will come to you. Think negative & negative things will come to you. Dream big! Claim big things! I am petrified of blood! Blessed are the poor. A rich man getting into Heaven is like a camel going thru the eye of a needle. Only scarred lives save. Religion can be witchery in the wrong hands. It is in the right hands with me. Mae is a sinner & a Christian reborn again Nicodemas bride of the Lord married to the carpenter Jesus Christ. Astrology is witchcraft. You had better take the bitter with the sweet. There is not a vain or mean bone in your body. You are devastated that Mary Marie's husband died of cancer - Humilities daughter class favorite. You are humble & you are meek Mae. The meek will inherit the Earth.

You are scared of sex per psychiatrist at Our Lady of Mercy. You cannot have sex with a catheter in your stomach. Fornication is a sin. Pray you do not need a new air-conditioner. Celibacy sucks!

Dream # 36

I am in a dark hell hole running around. There is a black afro man. There is a tent with a dentist with a bright light. I say I want to go home. The dentist says there are cottages. Uncle Humor & Aunt Wisdom are wearing bright white shirts a like trimmed in gold. They save me from the hell hole & I say who packed this bag.

Dream # 37

I am in a house. There is a half naked tattooed man. I am sitting outside with Zachariah. Mom is in the kitchen getting drunk. She goes to the car drunk with a lucky strike cigarette hanging from her mouth. I have to drive her home.

Dream # 38

Mom bought a huge nice house. My bedroom is really big. There is a chained-in fence in the backyard for the dog. There is a room with urine all over it full of people urinating on the gross floor. Mom is sitting at the bar drinking shots. She has money. I ask her if I can drink a rum & coke. She says, "Will it make you sick?"

Dream # 39

There is a nice clean new house out in the country for $56,000. I get in for half price. I have my German shepherd husky Calvin Klein & she runs to the next farm house & I am afraid he will shoot her. The kitchen is big white & clean & I am typing with a boy from Camel Carriers Trucking Company. He is a good-looking boy with 3 boys, 2 twins.

Dream # 40

I dream I am giving Isaiah the best sex riding him & we are going to get married. Sex is nasty. He is manic-depressive too & I should have married him at House of Horrors/ Wax at 24. Isaiah escaped with camouflage & helicopters were after him. He thought that was really cool & they put him in ICU. We used to write notes - New Jerusalem. Isaiah said Stevie Nix was jealous of him shooting him out of a limousine & he killed Bruce Lee. Was Mom scared of Isaiah on lithium? He was from Mayfield is married & has 3 girls & a boy. Did he pass down that manic-depressive gene? Deceased from a heart attack gay lesbian alcoholic SHIT all over you.

Dream # 41

Are you afraid of sex, Mae? With a catheter in your stomach for home kidney dialysis you cannot have sex - only dream about it. You are getting your teeth knocked down your throat for getting pregnant & aborting monk Lazerus's baby. That is murder. Sprinkle, sprinkle fairy dust Faith bitch! The devil made your mother shoot herself. Not today Satan. I dreamed I told Satan "I believe in God!" & he blew me backwards in my bedroom. Holy God, holy God hear my prayer. My sheepdog LEVI were in my brother's bed. I had a vision of a swaying Christmas tree & Satan black demon came & stole all the presents. Rev. Daniels said Satan was trying to steal your sanity. LEVI & I both saw the vision. God cannot stand that fat bitch Gracie Bathsheba in a wheelchair at Shop-a-Lot. She is a liar & a backstabber, talks about people awful & needs a shrink.

Dream # 42

When I was in Our Lady of Mercy, I saw stairway to Heaven in the clouds out the window. All you have to do is climb the stairs to Heaven. That is when a boy hung himself with a coat hanger. Dr. Sweden psychiatrist said he really wanted to die. Now, I would like to sue that doctor for putting me on lithium that shutdown my kidneys if he was not dead. Robin Williams who was manic-depressive hung himself. Did he go to hell? He used to make me laugh in Mork & Mindy. Nanu. Nanu.

Dream # 43

I had a dream I was at my grandmother's Mammy's house on Scott Street. I hugged her & she laughed calling me a wiggle worm. Mom was outside smoking a cigarette. I also dreamed I was at her house, I was 50 & the favorite & had to protect her. Firemen & police came in the house.

Dream # 44

When I worked at Mom's real estate office, I saw 3 black demons coming out of a fire in the wall after me that scared the hell out of me. I could have had a good job working at Zion, Egypt hospital, but, Mom was shorthanded & wanted me to stay. We used to go to the horse races, play cards, drink, eat, & be merry. God says there are dark spiritual wars. You had better have a sword! There are unicorns in Heaven.

Dream # 45

I am canoeing in a red canoe straight up a dirty river with gay Poinsettia strawberry blonde hair & blue eyes up to Heaven. I am in a clean institution with my back turned to Mon Loyal Dedication & her best rich red-headed brown-eyed friend, Maebelle. My hair is pulled back, blonde & down to my waist. I cannot see my face. I ask, "Where's Mammy, Wonderful Strength?" & they say, ok, she's around here somewhere in spirit.

Dream # 46

I was driving down Park Avenue & I had a vision of many candles in the sky. Mom flicked her bic lighter. Was your mother your best friend? Pray for your brother Micah a gay queer faggot. He has been a saint & he is cruel.

Sell the house & go into assisted living. He is full of bull SHIT. Faith without good works is dead. Your brown century Buick got stolen because you left the keys in it. They ran out of gas. Mom is telling you to stick the house Tara up your ass!

Anthony is a religious name. The Door of Hope is praying for you. Do you hear voices & do you want to hurt somebody kill somebody? You saw God spell on blue microdot acid L.S.D.

Lazerus is having flashbacks & he is so glad to see you in a half-way house in Heaven for suicides. Your life is in danger. Zion, Egypt in a very dangerous city. Pedifiles will go to hell!

Dream # 47

God cannot stand your Scorpio friend for putting you in Jebosite Haven & committing adultery with a man with the biggest cock dick I have ever seen. It was at least 13 inches long & hard as a rock. Her son just had a beautiful baby bear girl & they are doing well, fine. Do something out of the goodest of your heart. That was wrong! Hope nurse practitioner & Joy are mean Scorpios. Joy could not stand gay lesbian alcoholic Ecclesiastes. I took Ecclesiastes everywhere to eat, cut her hair, court & I expect to get blessed for it. I had a dream she was with me at Camel Carriers Trucking Company & my black Aveo Panther car got towed. She said the man was mean. You wish you could call her & probably get chewed out. Deceased Ecclesiastes can now see the hell you go thru with kidney dialysis every night.

Dream # 48

I had a dream I was walking my German shepherd dog
Calvin Klein - Snowden Zodiac Spy looking for Mom.
Karma who I don't like, Greece/Greek's wife was in the
dream. She won all kinds of awards in High School. I am
mad, at Godspell, Free Will's mother. Free Will is such
a jerk & Canaan wanted to give him poison ivy on his
birthday as a gag joke. Stay 6 feet away. They are both
bastards! Love one another as Jesus loved you. That is hard
to do some times especially when you've been abandoned,
betrayed & trespassed on. My books Jeans/Genes, AGORA,
Crazy Check, Queen Goddess of the Office are not stupid,
Micah has a degree in mixology - a bartender. This is what
an awesome brother looks like.

Dream # 49

How many people can you save? WWJD what would Jesus do? He would be mad with flowing white hair. Your body is your temple. Do something Christian per Juda Iscariot at Camel Carriers Trucking Co. Take mercy who died in a fire, busted for meth, get her catfish dinner & take her to your shrink. Her son accidently shot himself with a loaded gun & died. Sin told me that you want plastic surgery for your nose. How long do you have to live? In quietness & confidence is your strength. With God all things are possible. Take care of thyself!

Weebles wobble but they don't fall down. You had better not croak per that sweetheart social worker. You are a gray hound dog. All you do is puke up food on home kidney dialysis. It is scary. Theology my beloved tobby cat sees all the hell I go thru.

I dreamed I had a big dick & I touched it. I wanted to call my slutty friend & have sex.

Teston the Moleston at Shop-a-Lot went to prison for molesting raping his 12 year old cousin - a felony. He got into a fight & had a black eye. Teston the Moleston said the girls were pretty & tell them he had a big dick. I cannot stand spitting. Spitting is nasty. What is that black girl's name that used to make me laugh for cussing - Jasmine. You had better pray for your crazy family, Mae. Is your cousin Job drug mafia lord a pervert? You cannot be too young, too rich, or too skinny.

Dream # 50

Micah is a bitch & a mother _____er & he called the cops on those crazy gay guys. Was the gay guy doing meth & got evicted almost committed suicide twice. Micah said, "Oh, he's just doing that for attention." You would freak out if you found a squirrel in your house - Tara adobe abode. Squirrels are in the attic. How many people did Moses kill for worshipping a golden calf? You have seen Moses & he is very scary. How many of the 10 commandments have you broken, Mae? Candle, candle all aglow, tell me what you know. Is my house haunted with ghosts?

Dream # 51

I had a dream about Peace, the great art teacher, best friend of Mom's. She is so pretty with black hair & brown eyes & lived to be 89. Rev. Daniels says the dead people are alive & resurrected. She was an Aries, the greatest sign there is because St. Peter said Jesus was the son of God. Get thee behind me Satan! Was she agnostic? Peace was in a horrible car wreck, thrown from the car. The truck driver lost his leg. She got compensated for that. Are these ghosts in my house Tara? Are they friendly ghosts? Is God a jerk? No, He is mercy & loving kindness. Mom said you were going to be a snarley garley old lady - verbal abuse. How can you talk to your daughter that way. She told you to _____ off!

Dream # 52

You had better do everything that Holy Spirit/Ghost says to do. Spit those pills out in that dream. Get a ride in a clear box car. Call the police if there are pit bulls in your yard. Your spirit guide, the ghost keeps telling you to get out! Jesus can come back at any second. Don't be ugly in sharing with gay brother Micah. Homosexuality is an abomination of the lord. Do everything the great archangel says to do - Michael. Be careful what you wish for.

Dream # 53

I am a SCSM customer service manager at Shop-a-Lot. There is a red side & a blue side. I pick up a gigolo & we go to my apartment with a sunken living room & dance like in the 40's. He comes back the next day with candy & flowers & I have been shot in the head & die. There is a Mexican lurking in the hall. It feels good to die. Who killed me?

Dream # 54

I had a dream about Jayden "Care" Arthur at Shop-a-Lot. We were in a cafeteria with a long table. Gracie Bathsheba & Kindness are eating breakfast. I am looking for the ice cream scooper to feed my white cat Wrangler ice cream. Jayden is reading the newspaper. I say what is the coat & tie for? He says his mother died. I cry & he does not want me to go to the funeral wearing black. Jayden is adopted & his parents are 70 years old. Black means banishing evil.

Dream # 55

You saw LOVE in a dream when she o'd on morphine. She wanted you to have a drink with her. Mother was watching T.V. & could not sit down. I saw LOVE in another dream & I told her I had a nervous breakdown because of you. She is so mad you fell asleep when she was doing mescaline. The peace of strength, the strength of peace - 1974. It was all her boyfriend's fault that she died & now he is a lawyer.

Dream # 56

I dreamed I married Jayden in a white wedding dress gown & cried thru the entire wedding. Then I had on a lavender dress holding his hand. I am pregnant with a baby girl. His parents are talking about me. Ezekial & Jayden are having a foursome. He screws Ezekial's wife Ms. Mary USA & Ezekial is trying to screw me. Ezekial wants your money & Jayden wants your class. Ezekial hopes that Gracie Bathsheba dies. I am with Jayden & he gets off 7 times. I am in Our Lady of Mercy pregnant in a yellow printed maternity dress lying on the bed. The nurses say, "here's your Zyprexa." Jayden & Ezekial are visiting me & I jump up & sing karaoke.

Dream # 57

Charity & I keep going out & I keep losing my purse, my credit card is gone & I can never find my car. We are in a meeting with blue & purple grassroots at Shop-a-Lot. I cannot find my black Aveo panther car & I ask these nuns to pray. They said they were going to pray my mother comes back to Earth. I say no!

Dream # 58

I am with Jayden "Care" Arthur in his silver car. A truck hits us from behind & he is thrown from the car. Jayden broke his leg & I take off my shirt to wrap it to prevent him from going into shock. I get Mickey finned in Evansville & we go to a motel. We have sex & I do not remember a thing. He is a Taurus & I am an Aquarius on the cusp with Capricorn. He is too young for me. I am old enough to be his mother.

Dream # 59

I dream Micah my gay brother & I are over my beloved grandmother's Wonderful Strength's house on Scott Street & we have 20 minutes to get ready for school. I have to fold blue towels, white panties & put on mascara. Mammy was a seamstress born in 1900 & a Virgo 8-25 died in 1972. My whole world crashed. Germs, germs, germs. No good died goes unpunished. I worshipped the ground my grandmother walked on. The walking doll Suzzane Elizabeth is alive. She made beautiful doll clothes for her. Mammy could not stand drugs & that junkie nurse friend Japan of Moms. You know how to put an I.V. in Mae. Save a life & you know CPR. Pray your ass off! This is a sick, sick world. People are eating SHIT. Pray for Discernment your grandfather.

Dream # 60

I am a bride of the Lord & I get married in red robes. They are putting make-up on my face. I am married to a big bald headed man. I have 2 identical twin girls 2 years old- Molly & Polly & I want to have a boy - Scott Christensen - Scotch. When I got pregnant with Lazerus's baby, would Mom hit me in the belly? She was so against premarital sex. I dreamed Lazerus was up in Heaven in a half-way house for suicides. I visited him in a blue dress. I was riding a horse - brown with black mane & he was on a motorcycle looking for Jesus. Lazerus monk came back to me with a natural beauty girlfriend. There were zebra figurines.

Dream # 61

I have nightmares about the Amazing Marines soldiers of the cross. A girl bit my hand. The social worker is having sex with a black man. I leave the out of town apartment & go to the mall looking for cheese. Peace's beautiful daughter is there. I say you had better not sneeze if your appendix ruptures. I go back to the apartment & the van is gone. They have abandoned me & I get a ride back to Zion, Egypt with these 2 young good-looking boys. I offer to buy them gas.

Dream # 62

I have a dream about Canaan - lawn & garden. The town is named after him & his brother who I like. There are antique shops with pretty porcelain jewelry. I do not buy anything. He has a Capricorn girlfriend who is nice to me. I am so jealous. What do these stupid dreams mean? Girls gone wild is gross. Is Jesus a Capricorn or a Taurus? You are with Gabriel. Mae has been an absolute angel since God has talked to you.

Dream # 63

I am pregnant with a boy that looks like Micah, my gay brother - Brennan Scott Conner. Lutheran, the black classy lady from Camel Carriers Trucking Co. is there. Forgiveness & Lazerus's brother are there. Where is the father? I climb up a straight flight of stairs with the boy & we make it. Why say do you peace when there is no peace per Jeremiah? There are a bunch of dead people in your house, Mae. You cry every time somebody dies. Not today satan. Cleanliness is next to Godliest. I follow God's white-gloved hand everywhere. If you snap me out of this acid trip, I will never do it again! What if you thought you were possessed by the devil, shoot yourself like that dentist Fable did? You will go straight to hell for committing suicide. Say a prayer for the damned.

Dream # 64

On Mother's Day I had a dream. I was camping out with these 2 gay girls with a pit bull on blankets on McPherson Street. There is a girl with a container of chicken salad & I say I don't want it. I go back to the blankets & Mother comes down & says I am getting milk from the store. Do you want anything. I say get BBQ potato chips. I call my brother to wish him a Happy Mother's Day & he says, what the _____ does that mean?! Mother is dead! He absolutely ruined my Mother's Day & I go to Walgreen's South to buy BBQ potato chips in honor of my deceased mother. Mae is a helper. Mae is not a cold-hearted bitch. God likes your book. Be of good cheer, I have overcomed the world. All you have to do is believe. Whores make the best wives. Read those tarot cards - Queen of Penacles. My aura is magenta. All you have to do is "be. Have mercy."

Dream # 65

Thank you for your persistent candle - lighting faith I am coming down to save you from poverty & hate. These dreams seem so real or is it folklore? What is God trying to tell you? Be a cheerful giver. Call the cops to come & shoot this ghost. Get out of my house! Do not be afraid of the angels. What if St. Peter was by your bed? Give him the keys. He let you right into Heaven - streets paved in gold - reincarnation Mary Magdaline. Your like candy baby- hot, sweet, & sticky. These dreams are like flashbacks. How big is your umbrella? You cannot be a nun because you are not a virgin. A little birdie told you. Birds of a feather fly together. Aunt Abundance, a saint, said you weren't going to make it. That is so negative.

True/Trust/Truth said you will have to show her you will make it. Rich people getting into Heaven is like a camel going thru the eye of a needle. Gay lesbian alcoholic Ecclesiastes had a heart attack, died & she will get her revenge against Joy, Happiness, & Canaan. Mae is a prayer warrior. Hope flourishes. Doubt flees. When Jesus comes back, you had better get on those knees. Love, Gypsy Sky (Azul Celeste), the wicked get no rest. God is trying to warn you something in these dreams. Go to the library & learn. You are so blessed with clairvoyance, Mae. Faith without good works is dead. You are petrified of Scorpios. They rule the sex loins. Mae is so proud to be an Aquarius 1-21-58. My last dream, Mom & I are on a casino boat. There are a lot of pretty girls & I am handed multi-colored thumbtacks. Mom has a bible - the book of Loyal, Mae & Micah. I win the prize - the good-looking single casino man. We go in a room, make love, he presses his tongue on mine when we kiss. He said his girlfriend died in a car wreck & wants to marry me. I am 40. What does this dream mean? You are a power angel & you are killing every rapist. You are dancing & singing when you go to Heaven with the crown of righteousness. Jesus is the reason for the season. Don't tread on me. Beware of COVID-19.

Angel Unaware

I can see Angels everywhere
Floating over Earth, in the land, in the air
When I go to Heaven I will be
a power angel with a sword
Fighting dark spiritual wars for the Lord
White glowing beautiful celestial
beings with wings
Praising God & making Him sing
Protecting, guiding us all thru
the perils of the night
Do not be afraid of them full of fright
007 secret agents for Jesus Christ
Full of love, hope, faith, joy,
peace, glory, might
Fallen angel Satan Lucifer is
so conniving vain, 10,000
angels followed him
My best LEO girlfriend's
name was Kim
Look up to the Heavens above
& you will see an angel
unaware descending like a dove

Spreading God's word of peace across the land, the universe
Does God curse?

God is full of loving-kindness & mercy. His angels will
endure forevermore. Mermaids of the Lord, angels are sweet,
sandals on their feet.

Angels are answering prayers just as fast as they can Jesus
Christ is my man. Holy, holy, holy divine God's angels are
majestic full of glory

Do angels have sex? How do they reproduce? I can't stand
the name Bruce - born in a thicket. Mission impossible.
With God everything is possible. Pray till the answer comes.
Heaven or Hell. All is well. Follow God's white gloved hand.
What is your name angel unaware?

Dream # 66

I dreamed I was 8 or 9 months pregnant baby, asst. manager at Shop-a-Lot. I am in a yellow printed maternity dress lying on bed rest at Our Lady of Mercy. The nurses said, here's your Zyprexa. I did not want to take any drugs because I was afraid it would hurt the baby. Jayden & Ezekial visit me & I jump up & sing karaoke. The baby girl is 3 years old & Jayden hits me & breaks my jaw. The girl wants to live with me & all she says is I want a doggy. I want a daddy! He'll rape me. I am manic-depressive, paranoid schizophrenic, on home kidney dialysis. Pray for me. I do not want to get pregnant. The vision of the little girl has disappeared. I no longer hear her. I want a divorce. Theology, Juju, Dusty Engle, Felix my cats are my children.

Dream # 67

God owes you a big apology for scaring the living SHIT out of you. Count your blessings not your losses. Pray before you faint. Is the gun in your pocket at Shop-a-Lot # 666 # 999? God is my gun. Leah my cousin was whipped into religion. You were scared into religion. You picked your mother up & carried her to bed when she was passed-out in the hall floor. Your gay faggot brother did not do anything. You were exetrix & treated like a scapegoat. Mother said she was not fighting your battles for you when Tested Curse was talking about you like & dog. I am so tired of all this verbal abuse. I would fight every battle for my child. You saw France in a dream who died from cirrhosis of the liver at Camel Carriers Trucking Company. She had red hair & brown eyes & was very beautiful.

Pistol died from cirrhosis of the liver, Uncle Protection's nephew. I can barely walk with this catheter in my stomach & you had better not croak. I see dead people in my dreams - they are alive & resurrected in Heaven. Don't trouble trouble till trouble troubles you. Call a psychic. There's a crazy lady in that rocking chair. Are you playing possum? You are having a spell. Your mother & father both went to hell. Drugs are evil.

Dream # 68

I saw guitarist Gift/Gifted walking down the street with her beautiful long brown hair. She was a good Pisces, computer programmer for Camel Carriers Trucking Co. for 30 years, cat rescuer, green peace & did she die from cancer at 49? I was looking in my gray bomb car that I hated for cigarettes. I also had 2 more dreams about her. I would work for food. I am now disabled on disability for manic - depression, paranoid schizophrenia & home kidney dialysis. I feel like a worthless sack of SHIT. I only live for my books & for my cats. People that pray together stay together. Gift/Gifted was a talented green peace hippy & we used to smoke pot together & sneak out of the house at 2 a.m. & walk clear across town in the dark. I miss my good friend so much! Gift/Gifted was my best friend & just like a sister. I cannot go thru any more hell. All I do is sleep, dream, SHIT, pee, eat & take care of my cats - Theology & my black cat Juju - Hersheys Kiss Licorice. God, Yahweh, Jehovah will take care of you. Simplicity is the keynote. Acid is sorcery & you loved her father who had a glass eye from World War II 2. We used to play cards - spades, heart, rook & you had better know how many tricks are in your hand. Aquahlung by Jethro Tull who could really play the flute is a gross song. Everything in the Bible came true. You will be hated, desprised, put in jail. Christians will rise up against Christians. Is it the end of the world? Woe to pregnant women. I had a friend who almost died from having a baby & had to have a hysterectomy. The kidney people are treating me like a queen Goddess of the office. Pray for that financial waiver.

Dream # 69

You spat on cousin Faith's grave for aborting your child & telling you to go to the food bank. Aunt Abundance & Faith are such snobs. I had a vision in church that I was a scared Felix black & white cat thrown out of Heaven to save the world. You asked God for another day. The sand man is putting you asleep. Who's next to die? Micah is so spoilt rotten & Mammy cannot stand that gay boy for lying about whether mom's yankie friend was hanging around her. What are drugs? Pray for your best friend from church Hebrew Tabernacle. He has bad blood. I am so mad & jealous of my friend Charity. Her children paid for her air-conditioner to be fixed for $270. I had to pay $150. Charity is so lucky! Is it your medicine making you have these dreams?

Choose *LIFE*
(live-in-forever-eternity.)

What if you die in your sleep? This is the day the Lord hath made rejoice & be glad in it. I am broke. I am tired of all this bull SHIT bad luck. I am going to puke. Pray hard! Love yourself. You are going to shoot yourself. Say the Lord's prayer. Next door neighbor hurt my feelings when I asked if her son was retired from struggling on the stairs telling me not to ask any personal questions. MYOB Mind your own business. I cannot stand her horny Free Will's long skinny pencil dick with large piepan. He won't ask me out on a date. He just wants to come over & use me. They will not help me. Look at all you've done for them - turkeys, ham, food, trash, get groceries out of car, mail. Turn the other cheek. May that high class rich black man across the street will not help you. Only my gay brother Micah & Sagittarius Aaron can help you.

I love my cat Theo! I miss the misery. Jericho got fired from his heating company. Pray for him! Pray your ass off. You have got to stay alive to get Queen Goddess of the office published maybe, your books will be best sellers on Amazon. com. Maybe, they will make a movie out of them. Dream big! Claim big things! When you mess with SHIT you get SHIT all over you.

You are getting more responsibilities with this home kidney dialysis. I dreamed I was raped & murdered in a concrete apartment complex by a fat man. When I was going up to Heaven, Tawny Mae Harris was on the nightly news. I dreamed there was a man with slime green gonorrhea gross pus all over him. I decided it was time to quit having sex. I dreamed Persistance & I were in a boat in our swimming suits on a lake. Jayden appeared & she drove off. I said, yeah, he was really a snob.

I had beautiful long blonde hair with a boy & girl on my hips married to a doctor. I was not happy. He wanted me to fix standing rib roast with a thermometer.

I was waitressing in a restaurant smoking a cigarette. There was a pretty girl with beautiful long blonde hair. I said, "Are you my deceased friend, Persistance, a R.N. nurse?" She said, "Yes, I want to cut my hair up to here." I said, "don't cut your hair!" We were both very promiscuous. Faggots beware! God loves everybody. What is in that Gypsy Sky (Azul Celeste) crystal ball? Wear blue for psychic awareness. Is Mae clairvoyant? Candle, candle all a glow. Tell me what you know. You need help paying all these bills. Penance per Cheer. My deceased black soul sister. Do a good deed to make up for the bad you have done.

A great Aquarius born on Valentine's Day. I loved her! We are on cloud nine. You dreamed Cheer died & she died at 57 - so young. Oh, how I grieve. You can die from depression. Fight depression like a plague.

Dream # 70

You dreamed Mom was going to sell the house. You said
_____ you. She made a angry face & murmured _____ you!
back. You have your cat Theology to take care of. Aunt
Abundance appears at the mall & said now, now maybe
she'll change her mind. You cannot find your car in the
parking lot.

When we had the F5 tornado in November 2005, my
grandmother came & said 3 times, do not let your cat
Wrangler out. The cat wanted out so badly so I let her
out. Then your deceased Aunt Baba came & said, Mae go
outside & get your cat. I went outside & got the white cat
off the hood of the car & brought her inside. 5 minutes later
I hear a train

Dream # 71

I had another stupid, sick, sick gross dream. I had sex with my gay brother Micah. I took his medium hard dick & stuck it up my pussy. I said feel what pussy feels like. He said noooo! I must really be horny. There was a LIPS man with a large box. Have sex with him too. Mom & her junkie nurse friend Japan had a large dildo. Micah got that religious gay boy evicted. He used to send me religious healing cards. Almost committed suicide twice, went thru bankruptcy, had a job at the veteran's center with Alzheimer's patients, died from a bleeding ulcer bleeding from the mouth. I am devastated. Call the church & repent. Holy, holy, holy God Hosanna in the highest Blessed is he who comes in the name of the Lord. Hosanna in the highest.

Dream # 72

Sell the house & go into assisted living. Gay queer faggot Micah is so full of SHIT. He does not pray. All he does is feel thankful. Look what happened to Mary Marie's husband. He died from cancer. You learned that at the 56th class reunion. You have written 4 stupid books & you expect to get a discount from iUniverse for the 5th one - Hopes, Dreams, & Visions per God. Micah & Joy will pay for incarcerating me in Jebosite Haven at 50. I hope Hope Scorpio nurse practitioner dies. No smoking for 6 days - $6,000. I could not stand that Dr. Trojan. Do you think you are normal? Do you hear voices? They put you down and they tell you what to do. You are getting your but chewed. Look what that Lamictal did to you - suicidal tendencies. Hide the knife. Those voices are telling that lady to kill herself. That's been 14 years ago & you're still seeking revenge. Get out of my house! Does Micah have 6's on his head? You wished you had never read those LEFT BEHIND books. At Jebosite Haven, the crazy lady SHIT in the floor, married 7 times, & had no children. There was a wild Mon. Mon man singing in Jamaican. I have got to get out of here! What kind of horny dream are you having? You hate your mother's guts for calling you a slut! The Wiz was an awesome black play. Ease or down the road & that black nurse's son at the kidney place tap dancing is the most talented man I have never seen. Frank Sinatra who was in the mafia was my favorite - New York, New York, I've been a piper, a pauper- Job, my favorite cousin was selling oxycontin???. His son Sodom was selling cocaine & got shock probation. He was married to a devil woman & had 3 sons. I dreamed about this cheerleader friend who thought she was hot SHIT took my bag. Give me my bag back! It's got my driver's license & social security card in it. I pulled her hair. We are on a plane & Mom's junkie nurse friend Japan is flying it. She lands the plane & we are going to Santa Cruz in 15 days. I am on my period & I take the stinky tampon out & take a shower. Give me my bag back! This cheerleader got pregnant & the father would not marry her. She had a beautiful baby girl named Delia Helene. She was a photographer with a camera. I would name my child Fawn Christiana Mae or Christopher Scott. You & Lazerus was the perfect couple.

Dream # 73

I had a dream that I was at my house Tara adobe abode & a manager called me into the office at Shop-a-Lot # 666. He said you said Barbara Stovall has a dick. I did not say that! He showed me a picture of her. I said you fired me once you can't fire me again. Shop-a-Lot # 666 # 999 was an evil retail store full of liars & backstabbers. I love Jesus! You loveth much who forgiveth much. That fat bitch in the wheelchair is a liar. I quit! Gracie Bathsheba said if you're going to quit Brad the co-manager said to hand your vest in. Gracie Bathsheba lied. She makes me so mad! Capricorns & Aquarius do not get along. Don't trouble trouble till trouble troubles you. Gracie is going to file bankruptcy for her bone breaking disease. I thanked God for charity & financial waiver.

If we do not start loving we will start dying. Satan, Lucifer, diablo father of lies. He is spreading his vain wings & laughing at Christian's roaring around like a lion trying to devour & kill people. In your dreams you can never remember what days your English & history classes at Zion, Egypt Community College are on. Who sent you to Paul, a talented piano genius, con artist who was in jail for a year for drugs who died from aides or a stroke. God sent you. Sardines & oranges. Sex toys. Aunt Abundance rich bitch said, "did you _____ him?!" No, I did not. I was just showing him my beautiful calico guinea pig named Rainbow that I had for 4 years. You've got to pee urinate in your dreams & you get no privacy because you are on home kidney dialysis & COVID-19 is getting on your nerves.

You are a prayer warrior. Mae loves kangaroos, butterflies, humming birds, horses, zebras, dogs, cats, angels, fairies & money. You could have been raped, murdered when they broke into your house, Mae, & stole all your jewelry, lighters, church sacrament. The burglars could have set your house on fire. The police were young & dumb & did not do anything. Gypsies, tramps, & thieves. They could have stolen your T.V., killed your cat Theo. The religious laundry mat lady said that was bad & sad. Are gay people in the book of names? Homosexuality is an abomination of the Lord. You can love them just not like their ways. I can hear Mom's voice - you make me sick! I pulled her hair & told her to fix the god _____ door in a dream. Then there was this Pisces bitch who worked at the Amazing Marines soldiers of the cross that was busy.

Dream # 74

Sometimes, I have a good dream. I was working at Camel Carriers Trucking Co. typing on the whisper screen computer & it was very hard. There was a young girl crying with long brown hair. I said, baby don't cry. There were 3 tornados. Now, I am a worthless sack of SHIT on disability & home kidney dialysis. I was sitting at the park on a bench watching the ducks & geese mending my own business. In broad day light, a retarded man comes & sits down by me, puts his arm around me & asks me out. I say I am interested in someone else & he gets up, leaves, & drives off.

Dream # 75

I had a nightmare dream that I had a blonde cocker spaniel & we were going to a movie. The place was dark & not a place you would want to be. It was full of people with big dogs. I am holding my blonde cocker spaniel. Honey walking in the parking lot looking for my midnight blue car. Two mean men come up behind me & call me a _____ing bitch! I say I ought to slap the SHIT out of you! The short mean boy pokes me in the back. I start screaming, Police! Police! Help me! A young blonde girl shows up. I say they are bothering me. There are mean people in this world. I need help! Don't tread on me. An eye for an eye. A tooth for a tooth. You hear dead people. You had better do everything that Holy Spirit tells you to do. Get on your knees & say Lord have mercy. Mae is bitter.

Dream # 76

Micah, my queer gay brother ruined my Mother's Day. What the ___ does that mean?! Mother's dead. He does not care to hear my dreams. Is he in the book of names? I had a dream that he had 2 girls - Tessa & Jesse. There was a big spider in the living room. Micah picked it up & thru it outside. It was the most poisonous spider in the world. I was so upset & swing on the back porch railings slinging my long blonde hair. Do I live in a haunted house Tara adobe abode? I want the police to come & shoot this ghost. Beware of Argentina, Benjamin's heat, cooling, electrician's wife. Do you believe in Jesus Christ? I am married to him. Lay hands on me. Repent & be saved. Pray for her son Jericho that got fired. You told Micah to cram all his money up his ass & mother is telling you to stick the house up your ass where the sun don't shine. Do not be afraid of the light - orbs - deceased souls.

Dream # 77

Throw poker chips at Micah & make him cry. He is crazy not to pray. Be thankful! Something terrible is going to happen. Mae has got the 6th sense & shining. Do gay people go straight to hell? 2 men kissing & sucking dicks has got to be the grossest thing I have ever heard or seen. A man got shot & murdered for that from Carhartt. God is so sorry he scared you. In my dreams, I keep walking to my Aunt Beautiful Patience & Uncle Protection's house on Scott Street & asking him for a ride home. Uncle Protection said your mother Loyal Dedication treated you like SHIT.

Dream # 78

In real life, I am drinking red Moscato wine walking down the street looking for my black cat Juju. I was afraid she got run over. A boy comes up behind me & says, "Are you having an amazing day?" He is riding a skateboard & I say skateboards are dangerous. I ask him how old he is? 17. He said you have the body of a 26 year old. I say I am 64. He has hell boy tattooed on his chest, a cross on his arm, & home sick tattooed on his fingers. He says, "have an amazing day." Juju is alive. I dreamed that there was this white furnished farmhouse for rent to own for $78 a month - a deal too good to be true. I am very sleepy. It is good to have good dreams once in a while. I pray on my candle who I want to pray for & curse who I want to curse. Am I an evil queen?

My prayers are powerful & God answers every one. Dream big! Claim big things!

Dream # 79

I dreamed that I had a farmhouse & called Micah a dumbass. The girl cook down at the Amazing Marines soldiers of the Cross was cooking in my messy kitchen. There was a phone that turned into a lizard - red, green, yellow & if you stuck your finger in its butthole it would grow.

Dream # 80

I had a dream that there was a black man with a gun on my property & he shot a goose. I told him to get off my property & went inside to dial 911. The _____ing phone doesn't work! This is all the dreams I am going to write down. I hope you have enjoyed reading my book Hopes, Dreams & Visions per God as much as I have enjoyed writing it.

God shall give the angels charge over you to keep you in all your ways.

Psalm 91

He who dwells in the shelter of the Most High, abides under the shadow of the Almighty.

He shall say to the Lord, you are my refuge & my strength, my God to whom I put my trust.

Because you have made the Lord your refuge, & the Most High your habitation.

There shall no evil happen to you, neither shall any plague come near your dwelling.

For He shall give the Angels charge over you, to keep you in all your ways.

They shall bear you in their hands lest you dash your foot against a stone.

You shall tread upon the lion & adder, you shall trample the young lion & serpent under your feet.

Because He is bound to me in love, therefore will I deliver Him in trouble. I will rescue Him & bring him to honor.

With long life will I satisfy Him & show Him my salvation.

I am with GOD 24/7 even when I am asleep. Sweet dreams.

In the Bible, holy book, it says young men shall dream dreams & old men shall see visions. The wicked get no rest till they close their eyes for good. Are dead people asleep? Mae is on the prayer list at beloved Hebrew Tabernacle Episcopal Church - daughter of a King. WWJD- What would Jesus do? I am kin to the sleeping prophet Edgar Cayce by marriage.

Printed in the United States
by Baker & Taylor Publisher Services